Because of the Light

Because of the Light

POEMS BY ROSEANN LLOYD

HOLY COW! PRESS

DULUTH, MINNESOTA, 2003

Library of Congress Cataloging-in-Publication Data
Lloyd, Roseann.
Because of the light: poems / by Roseann Lloyd.
p. cm.
ISBN 0-930100-45-X (alk. paper)
1. Title.
PS3562.L76B43 2003
811'.54—dc21   200351056

Publisher's Address:
Holy Cow! Press
Post Office Box 3170
Mount Royal Station
Duluth, Minnesota 55803

This project is supported, in part, by a grant from the Outagamie Charitable
Foundation and by donations from generous individuals.

Holy Cow! Press titles are distributed to the trade by Consortium Book Sales
& Distribution, 1045 Westgate Drive, Saint Paul, Minnesota 55114.
For inquiries, please write us and visit our website: www.holycowpress.org.

This book is dedicated to my beloved
and the birds in the tree of life

In loving memory of Sheila and Paul Wellstone

Contents

Prologue

She Said   9

I **Midsummer**

The Midsummer Ghazals   13

Movement   20

A Summer Day   22

II **Winter Dark**

Resorting to Metaphor   27

Mørketiden: The Dark Time   30

Recollect   31

A Woman of the North Talking   32

Another Gift of the Northern Abolitionists   33

Field Trip: Kids from the Treatment Center Visit the Art Institute   34

Sorrow Comes in Spades   36

Falling Means You Have the Chance to Learn to Walk Again   39

Massage   40

Ragged but Right   42

The Winter Room Had No Windows but It Filled Up With a Lemony Yellow Light

III **In the Season of Chanterelles**

In the Season of Chanterelles   49

Walking Along the River Bluff, We Glimpse a Whir of Red Wings in the Brush   51

Blind-Sided   52

Midsummer in the Midwest   54

A Day That Starts Out Gloomy Turns Out Brighter than Expected   56

Still Point   58

Windows: Fall Equinox   60

Rose Quartz   62

iv Winter Light

Winter Light   65
What to Do the First Morning the Sun Comes Back   67
I Fell in Love with the Tropics   68
You Don't Have To   71
Santa Clara Convent, Antigua, Guatemala   73
¿Que Es?   74
Indigo   76
San Antonio Agua Calientes   78
How to Be Middle Class   80
A Dozen Reasons to Give Up Haggling over the Price of Weavings   82
Another View of Culture: She Explains Why She Loves Disney Cartoons   83
Poem on the Occasion of the Festival of the Immaculate Conception, Antigua, Guatemala, and the Confirmation of John Ashcroft as Attorney General of the U.S., 2001   84
In the Name of the Daughter   85

v Northern Sun

Natt og Dag: Return To Norway After 25 Years   89
White Nights: Another Woman of the North Talking   90
Summer Dinner Party in Oslo   92
We Didn't Have the Words Then   94
Lying Down in Public Places   96
The Color of Hills and Water   98
All I Knew about Wales Was That Grandpa Loved Ponies   99
The Woman They Found in Siberia   102

End Notes   104
About the Author   110
Author's Note of Thanks   111
Acknowledgements   112

She Said

the sun   she said   is the mother
of all living things   the plankton
in the oceans   the lichen
on the rocks   the wild magenta
roses   the reindeer
and the fish
                    every year   she said
the work of a hundred
women's hands brings the sun
back from Her winter rest
for the night is the mother
of the day
                    she said   let us name
these purple and yellow violets
Night and Day in honor
of the darkness and the light
let us name   these berries
Sun berries   these flowers
Owns-the-Sun and these
sweet wildflowers   *The Virgin Mary's
Golden Shoes*
                    put on your shoes
she said   your dancing shoes
your sturdy red tennis shoes
let the sun energy
come up through your feet
up from the warming earth
to your heart
                    yes   she said
your heart   with its emerald shimmer
the color you see in the summer
on the underside of waves

I

Midsummer

Midsummer Ghazal: July 1

The smell of rain came down the chimney before the rain.
Only in summer do we get to see yellow sky.

All day long the heat had weighed on me like a musty shroud.
If I don't get my period soon, I said, *this throbbing vessel will burst.*

One friend said, *You can tell a woman's age by her neck and hands.*
Another friend, *Never mind all that—put some yellow roses in a crystal vase.*

I look in the mirror and see a woman I do not know.
What does she want? *Gold,* she says, *for my new freckles.*

Last week she went shopping for a shell-pink scarf.
Then: walked along the freeway without sunscreen.

Funny how you can smell a change before it comes.
The eyes of the yellow daisies under the freeway stare like deer.

Once I struck the poet's pose by the stone tower of Robinson Jeffers.
My neck was sleek as a pony's, ocean salt in my silver mane.

In the night, my dream of bleeding asks, *Is this the end of it, then?*
What new life swirls in the lavender tide pools at Monterey?

I can't believe how sweet the black amber plums taste this year
and how, when I go to church, tears run wild down my face.

My heart is open, my past blown away.
The wind brings roses mixed with the smell of rain.

Midsummer Ghazal: July 2

In the ghazal, I said, *each couplet should stand alone.*
Each line, half of a jeweled bracelet. In honor of Persia—and of love.

I was watching the sky as I talked, through five high windows.
Blue. Gray. Jade green. Yellow. Navy blue. Five tones.

The ghazal thrives on non sequiturs, I said.
The wind was thriving on the pale underbelly of resisting leaves.

The students, intent on poetry. I kept talking, though I didn't want to.
The sky was time-lapse photography without the lapse.

How old are you when you watch a storm? I'm always six.
Watching my dad watch rain-black trees show all their arms.

Let the wind blow through the empty spaces of your poems.
My students frowned. My example didn't follow the rules.

If you don't want to observe the old rules, make up new—
instead of rhyming, braid a pattern of thunder and gold.

It has always been a relief to me that God comes in the wind.
I need to empty my heart of bitterness, as well as my brain.

All the light went out of the sky; lamps came on in the room.
It was quiet except for the scratching of pens.

The ghazal works against narrative; but this is the story of a class.
Did they find me a lunatic? Is this a non sequitur?

In the morning, the TV showed lakes where streets had been.
Straight-line winds had tossed trees like matchsticks, rows and rows.

Midsummer Ghazal: July 19

Morning, the house shut up against the heat.
Only thunder can wake me.

In my dream last night, a baby boy filled my arms.
I crave the smell of babies, even though I'm past all that now.

Yesterday, a friend told me her sons play soccer all summer.
They won't come with me any more to see the baby animals at the zoo.

*All that testosterone...*she said.   Every letting go has a new picture.
If, in my dream, I'm making love with my ex, have I forgiven him?

When it thunders, you understand silence.
In all my college classes, no one spoke of Zi Ye.

I've completed many ceremonies, designed to release bitterness.
Only when you dream a release   is it real.

My ex lay directly over my heart, in midnight blue.
He was inside my heart, tiny, and life-sized, both at the same time.

The spider web in the sunny window has caught 100 raindrops.
My friend said, *Keep my crystal vase. Use it for your roses.*

Midsummer Ghazal: July 20

First the heat kept me indoors, now the storm.
Thunder cracks the southeast then the north—rain comes sideways.

Yellow pillows, left on the porch, soak up the sky.
The black-capped chickadee does not turn upside down, feeding.

I'll shape my day around the weather, stay in bed and read.
Lotions will do their work on the soles of my feet.

They say lavender oil brings a sense of peace and well being.
Was it the flowers that changed the tyrant in *The Secret Garden*?

Dew point 73: I want to nap all afternoon.
At night, my appetite for talk and chicken flautas will return.

Once a shaman—in a sequined sweatshirt—read my aura.
Yellows, she said, *need sex, exercise, and meditation on a daily basis.*

The bronze Buddhas from Cambodia smile with their eyes closed.
Their skin still glows after 1,000 rainy seasons.

The thunder cleans the air of heaviness, and the past.
Once a barefoot girl ran through tall, wet grass.

Walking is its own meditation.
After the rain: puddles, crickets.

Why did I ever deprive myself of roses?
All the way to heaven is heaven.

Midsummer Ghazal: August 18

Where the lake and river meet, water lilies open every morning.
The loons scoot about: calling, diving, circling like bumper cars.

My grown-up girl bobs up out of the water like an otter.
Brown and wet, sputtering sounds, oil, droplets—

Remember the thunderstorm when the canoe got stuck in the reeds?
Remember the summer it was so hot, dead fish piled on the beach?

Remember when we made Rice Krispie bars over the campfire?
You know you're old when your children want to reminisce.

The woven Oriole nest swings in the wind, empty now.
When she was two, she held a teaball, said her first word: bird.

A doe and her fawn graze on flowers that match their gold coin spots.
Sometimes synchronicity happens only for our pleasure.

All night last night I was busy sorting out wooden childhood toys.
My girl took me by the hand: *You don't have to do that any more.*

Once I was discouraged, holding her.
Purple fingernail polish, anger enough for three lifetimes.

On Star Island, she found a meadow in a perfect circle of birches.
Life, fragile as the lavender dragonfly at my feet.

The thing about summer is—it's gentle.
You can go in and out of the house without tensing up.

She curls up to sleep like a big kid.
In a tangle of snakes, headphones, rose and pink peonies.

Midsummer Ghazal: August 20

The monarchs are staging like orange clouds in the white pines—
Do the milkweed blossoms or the stars guide them to Mexico?

The fuzzy bees are landing only on spires gone fuzzy.
The ferocity of day lilies: tiger gold, ruby, russet, yellow, cream.

My old yard has grown into woodland.
Dark lavender shade of birch and cone flowers.

Last year I walked the labyrinth. For the first time in my life
I felt compelled to bow myself to the ground.

Some say summer has flown away.
But the loons *yi-eee* through the wind, through waking and sleep.

Everything has its timing. Once I felt the waves move
inside my spine, three minutes up, then the still point, then down.

The center of the labyrinth is an empty flower.
Do we, then, circle like bees in Her honor?

There's a great comfort in letting gravity hold you.
Living the season as it is, hot, muggy, dull.

To attract juncos in August, throw sunflower seeds on the ground.
To ward off the void of winter, stew plums, ginger, and mangos.

I have seen the Queen of Heaven in the black summer sky.
I have heard her pass in the hush after thunder.

At this age, there are a few things I know for sure.
One: I'll never be Bonnie Raitt in this lifetime.

Last night in my dream I discovered my brother's black saxophone case:
a lost velvet treasure, filled with tiny silver toys and charms.

At the labyrinth there was a crescent moon.
The wind brought the earthy cricket's song inside.

We still have another month before the wild geese fly away.
The sunlight in the water is turning all the rocks amber.

If they ask, what is the sign of the one who sent you, answer:
It is a movement and a rest.

The black tea steams the kitchen with blossoms of rose and jasmine.
I am being gathered by a levity that holds its ground.

Movement

for Jessica

the way the full moon   sinks to the bottom
of moving water
playing with small white stones

the way the golden finch   scallops
through the canopy
of the cornfield

the way the hill   behind the farm
curls up on itself
the roots of trees   visible
above my line of vision from the porch

the way the field of clover   opens
across the pasture and down the hollow—
purple

the way the clouds   turn
at sundown
indigo   from West Africa

the way the dark cerulean clouds
move the smell of rain   down
between the dark V of the hills

the way the night wind   lightly
fans through the black
screen porch   cicadas

the way the hill shadows   blacken
into shades of green:
dragonfly belly   snakeskin
bracken

the way they told us in grade school
to color the sky   sky blue
not the clouds

the way I got into trouble
for coloring clouds blue   anyway
and for outlining my pictures
in my favorite color   black

the way it's taken me forty years
to see   the blue clouds rising
from green shadows

the way the blue clouds rise
from the moving water
with the moon

A Summer Day

Central Park, New York, New York, June, 1991

A tall man dressed in a black tux
and a red bowtie
stands smiling, glancing
at the ginkgo trees above him
and the people strolling by.
At his feet, a tiny man
dressed in an identical tux and tie.
No kidding! They have the same slicked back
black hair and the same twirly mustachios!

The tall man is smiling and nodding.
The tiny man is playing a violin—
playing a Viennese waltz
so familiar its name is on the tip
of my tongue even now.
The violin is so tiny
even a cat could play it
if she so desired.
And the bow, the tiny bow!
calling forth a throaty resonance
a confident 3/4 beat.

I want to see the resin box
for this bow, the closet
where the tiny man folds his clothes,
his silver rack of polished party shoes.
There are strings, of course,
tiny blond strings on the fiddle and the bow,
and black strings taut
from the tiny man's back and arms
that rise to the intricate cat's cradle
in the tall man's hands,

the man who isn't looking at his hands,
who looks into the trees and nods.
I'm not paying any attention to those strings
nor to the tall man's nodding smile.
I can't keep my eyes off the music.

I can't take my eyes off the music, the tilt
of the head, the swoop of the bow
I am swaying ONE two three ONE
two three, ready to waltz away on the grass,
hoping I don't embarrass my friend
who doesn't want us to act
like the midwestern hicks
that we are, my friend who has been walking with purpose
towards the art museum across the park.

At the rising end of a good sway she suddenly
pokes me—*There's a record player, you know,*
and, yes, I know, I know, I see it there behind
the tall man's feet,
a little record player that folds up
into a tan suitcase, brass fittings on the corners
and I'm nodding, speechless, *Yes—I know—*
I see a record player—I see
another life I could've led…

Of course I would've had to be born
a boy, a physically coordinated boy, I would've
had to move here long ago, while they still
had rent control, abandon my friends, sure,
maybe my kid, too. But what a life! Playing
a violin in a sunny park, where Chinese women still
come to gather ginkgo nuts to roast
before the snows set in.

This waltz event so much more fun
than morose Strawberry Fields we just surveyed,

so much more fun than the art museums, the
antique stores in SoHo, more fun even
than the Indian curry restaurant,
my designated favorite tourist site.

And no matter where you go, there's always someone
pulling the strings. Always someone announcing
that pleasure is an illusion, death on the way.
Are you going to let that stop you? Stop you
from swaying to the music?

I shake my head like a two-year-old
and dig in my pockets for all my shiny dimes.
Toss them into the tiny red velvet violin case
open on the sidewalk.

II

Winter Dark

Resorting to Metaphor

for Sandy Larson, who got off a plane from Indonesia one January
and announced: Minnesota is exotic

I
43° below   not counting wind chill
the roads are chalky I say   it's the kind of day
that causes us to resort to art—
even the simplest metaphors—
to describe how unnatural *nature* is:
we take umbrage we are amazed
at her extremes

the roads are chalky I say again
a giant hand has taken a fat piece of pastel
and made sweeping
arcs across all the roads

and the cars are scurrying like bunnies
through the snow scatters—
the horizontal sweep of wind

maybe the word *bunnies* is going too far but
the roads are still chalky like the time
I took my kid aged 6
to the Picasso exhibit she scorned
the painting of his son
holding a pencil or a stick
making chalky marks on a navy blue slate:
that boy scribbles she announced
she couldn't see the art for the affront
of it: its betrayal of everything
in human life that is right and true

her stance the opposite of my chalky roads
where the categories of art and nature
continue to misbehave as I head across
the Mississippi River bridge:
the steam off the river
rises like the steam bellowing out
of the giant's tea kettle

I'm making myself a fine giant story here
with tea kettles whistling and
we'll have a fine feast of our own today
at Dim Sum after the panel
we'll talk a mile a minute and eat up
steaming sesame dumplings with lotus
hidden inside: so lavender
you wonder if it's food or not:
soft as ice cream but hot

my friend—the smartest critic I know—will be wearing
electric blue high heels—velvet!—
she will light on the crystal sidewalk
like a unicorn in a child's picture book
next to the story of the giants in the clouds

the poem about swans
I read with morning coffee before leaving the house
passes with me over the chalky roads
over the river bridge   passes
with the steam and food and friends
the musical insistence of their wings

2

living alone for the first time in my life
I love to scurry around town
on Saturday
even in winter over the chalky roads

my daughter   on her own
has discovered the solace
of artifice

after the summer teal

she has dyed her hair dark red
the color of mahogany
from Indonesia

last night I had to drive by her house
just to look at her

Mørketiden: The Dark Time

Now that you have fallen into the winterdark,
you believe those ancient stories of the North—
how all forms were once immanent
in the ice: protozoa, trees, lichen, people, dragonflies—
coming to life
only when the giant cow licked them free—

Now that your blood is flowing away from your limbs
preparing for the rites of human sacrifice—fingers first, and toes—

Now that your brain itself feels stupid & dead
as dead as a Celtic mummy in a peat bog
the rope around her neck still as taut and delicate as the insects
frozen in amber with her—

Now that your brain knows it has been sacrificed
for her master, the heart,
where all the vibrations of the Northern Lights
center their energy, blood blue as snow in the winter light—

Now that the heart *is* master of your body
with her ponderous breathing, her half moons glimmering
on all ten of your nails—

Don't worry about time passing, about
your plans, your future. Enjoy this
suspension of time. Cut out red and gold
paper stars. Light globes
of candles. Simmer a dark root stew.

Any minute now: You'll hear a snuffle,
a snort. Any minute now, that fat warm tongue
will be licking you
on your cheek.

Recollect

for Julie Dash

She gave us reindeer hearts in a rich dark sauce
pungent with the tang of *tyttebær*—in awe
of the table, we feasted:
roasted salsify roots, potatoes, cod roe with
heavy rye bread chewy as meat.
Afterwards: black coffee boiled up with egg.
Cloudberries, amber, floating in cream.

She said, *When you are far away from me, when
your limbs are scattered, remember our feast.
Remember. Recollect. Recall. The heart
is a muscle that always works.*

We went out into the world well-fed.
Crossed the jagged terrain, sure-footed,
knowing where the snowy ground would hold, where
it would give way. We traveled distance with ease,
reading the lichen and the stars. Summers,
we savored the Blue Hour, went down
to the sea for salt. Our deer, following, made beds
for themselves in the tall beach grass.

And now when our granddaughters weaken,
when they fall prey to the bleak city lights—
discouraged by double shifts, carpal tunnel,
disheartened by beatings, threats of death—
we whisper to them in the dark: *The heart is a muscle*

*that always works: Recollect. Remember. Recall:
how she led us down to the sea, how
she taught us to hold our ground, how to keep
going in the face of loss, how she
gave us reindeer hearts in a rich, dark sauce.*

A Woman of the North Talking

That was the happiest time of my life, the time
I spent working on Svalbard, even though
winter there is total darkness, white on white
landscape, rolling shapes of hills, no trees.
Happy alone, even though I had to carry a rifle
at all times, you know, because of the bears.

The amazing thing about that place is
any time you step outside, there's a chance
you'll see the Northern Lights—that ecstatic
electrical movement of life. Outside
in the dark, you sense
the mystery of the sky, of the continents shifting,
the earth opening up
like a flower. It's no surprise
to see fern fossils in the rocks. The tropics—
where we first came from.

Once before I left to go back
to the architect firm on the mainland,
I went out to a wilderness cabin,
went out alone—hiking. Knew
there were bears around.
Could sense them tracking me.
They're hard to see of course—white
bears on white snow. At the cabin,
their tracks by the back door—white on white
paw prints—spirits almost. Inside
I didn't dare start a fire and cook—
that smell would draw them back to me.
I ate some canned meat, cold,
went to bed with the rifle.

Safe—
alone with myself.

Another Gift of the Northern Abolitionists

I was a child with a gift for words.
My heart longed for books, more books—notebooks and pens.
My sister was the artist in the family, allowed to draw
on Papa's library walls—he had dreams
of changing the world. I also longed

for justice. I wanted to be a soldier
for the North. They made me be a nurse
because I was a girl. I didn't have many adventures
after the war, though, for I never recovered from the mercury
that slipped like a silver snake through my body,
killing off the typhoid fever—and God knows what else.

I don't know why I never married. Henry at supper
was company enough, I suppose. I am not Jo,
the ebullient woman I created, manager of that large
and rambunctious family, and a writer, besides.
I'm a small, retiring woman in a plaid taffeta dress.

My first novel never published—
they said it was too racy for a *lady* to have written.
Too racy! Too unlady-like! I have little to show
for my efforts. And so I'm still here, in my childhood home
in the orchard. In my room, I have two writing tables,
something precious in a time when many cannot read.

For two decades now, I have been left
with a weakened constitution, and a courageous mother
who has been angry every day of her life.
I keep writing any way. At least the mercury
did not take my thick dark hair.

Field Trip: Kids from the Treatment Center Visit the Art Institute

We are sitting and staring at the mandala made of sand,
me and the kids, quiet. *Yamantaka: The Realm
of Pure Form without Desire.* Winter white outside,
this realm is anything but quiet—blue and red
and yellow, electric colors, lightning bolts, tigers
and flowers. This is the mandala the Tibetan monks made,
the very one that the local 3M chemists glued together
with a special glue they invented
solely for this ludicrous purpose:
hanging sand on the wall of a museum.
Sean and Josh are desperate to climb the fence,
finger the sand but they show remarkable restraint
and bump and bop on each other instead.

We know that there was another mandala
which was properly disposed of, according to Buddhist practice:
Focus, release. Last fall, my friend Stephen drove the monks
with the real mandala to the Lake Street Bridge
where they let the bright sand slip like a waterfall
down to the river below.

Now all of us are laughing, wondering if *looking* at the glued
mandala will bring a death curse upon us. God knows,
these kids have had enough curses in their lives.
Battery, assault, rape, torture, you name it. It takes
a lot of pain to make an addict at age fourteen.

They start to wander, their assignment: to find something
really cool & write about it. Amy stands for half an hour
in front of a white jade bowl from China
polished until luminous. It could elegantly
hold a dozen pink peonies. Whimsically,
it offers dog heads for handles so that a young girl

could lift it easily, carry it to her room.   Amy's shirt sleeves
cannot cover the slashes on her arms, metal staples
from the ER holding her skin on her bones.
She turns, breaks her trance. Throws back
her long biker hair. *I have to walk away now*
so I don't get attached and all that shit.

Amy's abrupt gestures mimic
how my ex-lover turned
away from me. His ancient, hidden scars.
Neither 3M nor the Emergency Room—
neither the mandala nor the art museum—
was of any use to me then. They say scar tissue
is the devil's tissue and I know for a fact
this is true.

But here today I've found a path beyond pain
through this child with silver staples cascading
down her arms. I turn and enter the Realm
of Pure Form without Desire. Lift and
release the red and blue sand
from the Lake Street Bridge.

Watch it stream like a lavender waterfall
to the glittering river below.

Sorrow Comes in Spades

for Paul and Sheila Wellstone

cold today third coldest october
in history but it's my annual fall cold—
'tis the season, i say in my bathrobe,
drink hot ginger tea, turn to morning
email   john's daily nature poem
talks about toads spading down
five feet   home below the ice
if only we were so lucky
to dive down safe

the season is progressing as expected
downward to the solstice

spade, what a good verb, i say, forward
it on, dive into my students' portfolios—
CNN my white noise for reading
poems, writing notes about the
beautiful work, knocking down
Patrick's grade for missing
the second poetry reading even
though he gave me his bus transfer

the season is progressing as expected
downward

now CNN is saying the sniper battered
his ex-wives, threatened to end their lives,
refused his children all food except
crackers, honey, and vitamins,
and reporters ask *but were there any signs
he would do something like this?*
the police are spading up his yard

the season is progressing as expected
downward

the sniper is caught we're back to
showdown iraq my students
praise each other's poems: *egg-spinning
equinox,* the young man who's
failing my class for skipping
asks in his excellent anti-war poem
does anybody care but me?
sorrow ices my heart

the season is progressing as expected
downward to the solstice

plane down in eveleth freezing rain
hits the plane in spades   the season
is progressing but it's too early
for plane crashes in the jack pine
marshes too early for iced-up wings,
an unexplained *pop* even if this
is the third coldest   no, the season is

not progressing as expected   words

words crash about   some pilot
flies over the wreck says   he says
the numbers on the tail the numbers
are the same as wellstone's
plane i see it hitting the earth
like a spade *jim,* i dial, *paul's
plane is down   please come
home early it's hard to cry
alone* for a few precious moments
i hold out hope for sheila

the season is progressing as expected
downward to the solstice down

our bravest citizens, our happy
warriors, the ones
who wear our hearts on their sleeves
have gone to earth, too early, have gone—
gone to ground

where we will find our hope?
messages burned in ice

Falling Means You Have the Chance to Learn to Walk Again

for Corinne

She was quiet as she worked on my injury,
my left side weakened by a long ago fall
down basement steps. Suddenly my thigh
turned into dry ice, my feet roasting
before a campfire. I knew from before
she'd say, *Cold means a deep release*
but I didn't expect her
to pull on my feet, to traction them,
to balance left and right. I didn't expect her
to stand quietly at my feet, holding the length
of me: *I'm seeing diamonds—every cell
of your body filled with light. You don't need
to be afraid of the pain.*

At that moment, although we didn't know it
at the time, it started snowing.

Later, at home, I stood in my kitchen
drinking water. I watched the snow
filter sun on an icy branch—making diamonds—
and diamonds on the black thistle seeds
in the bowl of the feeder

waiting for the birds
who bob their heads
like newborn babies, the ones
who've been dipped in strawberry juice.

Massage

for Deet Lewis

Your arm is my baby now, she says
and my arm is suddenly hovering
over the surface of a lake, my skin
lavender, a dragonfly above water.

My baby, she says again
lifting up one of my legs
and the dragonfly
morphs into my baby so long ago—

Her first bath: on a navy blue towel,
in a kitchen sink,   the warm water
only an inch deep. I slowly let her down
into the water, cupping her head…

When she felt the warm wetness,
she turned her head, startled, looked
straight into my eyes. Some say
a week-old baby's eyes do not focus

but I do not believe this. She did not move
any part of her body, then, except her eyes,
making her first small frown. *What is this*
strange world I have come into?

I must have looked puzzled in that same way
when I woke up in the hospital
last year, saw her standing above me
golden as an angel. I could not figure out

for the life of me what the two things were
sticking up at the end of the bed.
I could not make my mouth say words,
could not ask about the wires

under my shirt. The angel said,
You're going to be fine, Mom.
Do you want me to take off your sandals?
Her voice, a soothing mother voice.

How can I bear to leave her?

Ragged but Right

after learning of the death of the musician Dave Ray

Karen's poems sing to us her sister's waltz and tango,
the tap of high-heeled boots, Garfunkel's hands. In her story,

a depressed young man on a city bus meets a woman
who changes his life. The class debates: *Can one*

stranger change your life? Memory gives me
one answer: the Triangle Bar, during a war,

Koerner Ray and Glover, amber cold bottles,
sawdust on the floor. The man next to my husband

says, *Why aren't you listening to her? Hey, man,*
this beautiful woman? I didn't know about narcissism.

Dave Ray gone now, and that husband, that brother,
that stranger whose words, later, come to comfort me.

Maybe my brother knew his name.
Now I'm the one who listens. Karen leans in close,

so the rest of the class won't see her tears.
If I miss the rehearsal, my professor won't let me sing

in the Christmas concert and I won't pass the class
but if I go to rehearsal I'll miss your class. God knows

I'm strict about attendance—but not a fascist.
Of course we'll work it out.

I tell her a story about a friend
who skipped out once, didn't go back to singing

for 30 years. *You need to sing,* I say. Karen
laughs, finally, says choir directors are maniacs

who think students have no other tasks. Her voice
hoarse with her love for music and anger

at her director: *It's only singing.*
And our task in life? Leave some kindness behind.

Only singing.

The Winter Room Had No Windows
but It Filled Up with a Lemony Yellow Light

For Corinne

I

The stalk is thick & strong, it's holding
a green cap that's holding a large round head
which is as big as a gourd, carrying many seeds
across its face. Little points
grip the head securely—the head is a little elf
sporting a green cap.

Magically, gravity has gone away & the head,
the capped head, floppy, moves to its own
sensations of wind & sun & air. The head
turns gracefully in the air—eyes not yet open
yet seeking the warmest direction—turning
with irregularity up to the sun, rising
higher with each turn. Spiraling, dipping
the head wants to burst forward
to the sun, burst forth its thousands
of seeds—what it has to give to the future—
& as it does so, as it makes
its bursting forth,
there's a sensation of tightness, the elf cap
constricting movement forward—the green points
gripping, pulling back so tight
that the eyes wrinkle—

a wave of feeling sweeps over the head, its first
fear: *Does it hurt so much to be born?*
With the question comes the impulse to not
burst forth, to pull back inside the cap, points closing over,
erasing the sun. This, the impulse to stay
in the world of dampness,
drawn shades, hateful words, the same chess game
played over & over.

But, no. The desire to live is too strong.
Inexplicably, the head
bobs up in the wind, dancing in the sun.

2
Much later, the head learns it has a body,
not just a trail of tendrils, vines, flopping foolishly
behind it, & below it, jellyfish fashion.

Someone has tucked the sheet around its shoulder.
Someone has put a pillow under its knees,
swaddled its legs with soft flannel.
Someone has been gently singing old songs.
Someone has cradled the head's body in all its length.
Someone has rubbed oil on its forehead.
Someone has laid his heart on its heart.
Someone has said, *I'm glad you were born.*

Now the head has attachments—
appendages, hair, torso, heart, stomach—
a body! There was a body there all along,
a heart that needed more listening room,
more attention to its glistening golden sac,
legs that needed to walk, blood
coursing the pathways in between.

Now the head is not alone.
It has attachments.
The green stalk holds it steadily.
Now the head can take a break, can
let the heart do the thinking, let
the pelvis settle down, let the arms
take charge of the rhythm of the day.

Now the head is free to nod in the sun,
to move with the clouds
& bees & the ruffles
of breeze & when the sun moves far away,
as it will, the seeds
the head has carried will fall free. The birds —
the cardinals, the chickadees & jays—will alight,
will carry off the seeds
to start more life

without any effort at all.

III

In the Season of Chanterelles

In the Season of Chanterelles

after Rumi

for Ilze Mueller, translator, poet, forager,
who names the seasons by the food she gathers

In the season of chanterelles, I discovered that every full moon
rises the moment the sun is setting,

that mulberries leave a cosmos of purple moons on the sidewalks,
that you can find most anything you need at yard sales: raffia, teapots, pillows,

that this summer is the hottest summer in 600 years and
cranky callers argue with the long message on my answering machine,

that your Teacher may come in any form, a mirthful girl from North Dakota,
that your Beloved may appear in church one day, to read a poem 700 years old,

a poem by Rumi that opens your heart, like all the Rumi poems you know by heart:
Inside the great mystery...

✿

In the season of chanterelles, I discovered that every full moon
rises over the freeways as slowly as over the open fields,

that when my Beloved stopped to pick mulberries & put them in my mouth
cells all over my body bubbled up to be fed. I discovered

that I didn't want him to stop.
That's what I said the first night I was with him: *I don't want you to stop.*

That's how I knew I was falling in love, my voice was husky when I talked.
I'd heard him singing behind me, before I'd turned to look in his eyes.

Walking to church, we followed the purple moons on the city sidewalk.
Only in Persia, Rumi's homeland, do people still make mulberry jam.

🖋

In the season of chanterelles, I discovered that ancient desires
rise up with the summer moon, with the sounds of cicadas, window fan,

that I like the texture of my hands
rubbing grape seed oil on the soles of my Beloved's feet,

that I like to wake up early, for the first time in my life,
to steam strong coffee, to pour batter into a hot black skillet

to roll the pancakes up with yoghurt & mulberry jam
to imagine lovers at breakfast in Montana, Persia and Israel—

I discovered that Rumi built a tomb for his cook, that my hands
are still supple, in the ancient ways of cinnamon, cumin, and oil.

🖋

In the season of chanterelles, I discovered mulberries have been here all along
holding their musky purple under the full full moon,

that hunters won't say where they find the chanterelles, they'll only give you hint
Look for huge oaks with long, sparse grass underneath…

that mulberries are easy to find, even in the middle of the city:
Walk on Lake Street, just around the corner, to Bill's Import Foods.

I discovered that what we need is always here, waiting.
Through patience the mulberry leaf turns to satin.

I discovered that inside my rush of work & freeways, there is a quiet room,
that *dervish* comes from the Farsi root for *door.*

🖋

I stepped out of the entryway into a courtyard sunny with lilies and marigolds.
I discovered again my own muffled ecstasy: In the season of chanterelles.

Walking along the River Bluff,
We Glimpse a Whir of Red Wings in the Brush

After Rumi, Poem 1246

And have we been there, all along,
inside the cardinal's radiant song, *Hey…*
hey…come on, come on, come on,
come on? Have we been inside that song
that rises from the yard where iris
rise in purple bloom? Have we been inside
the dark and shaded room, inside the night winds
that stir the whirring window fan? Have we
been inside the smoke that rises
from the sweet grass in the moon-
shaped ocean shell, in the dark room turning
pale? Have we? Have we been there
all along, inside the cardinal's full
and throaty call at dawn? That call
that makes me want to rise
to you inside me, me inside your arms? Inside
that song, inside? Have we been inside each other
all along? Inside the dark room
turning pale, inside the sweet grass and the wind,
inside the whirring window fan, inside the iris
rising into purple bloom, inside
the hollow of the red
full-throated song—
have we been there all along?

Blind-Sided

for James Wright

The first week after we'd met, your face
and your name kept slipping away—
faces from the past floated up,
caught wide-eyed, deadheads
in the river—I tried to focus, to
bring you back: the width
of your shoulders I'd reached around,
your hands on my waist.
      I'd sensed
already the full measure of you. Surely
I could picture your blue-gray eyes.
But, no, all that came to me was
your voice, *I like it when you're walking*
on my blind side.
      Saturday, when we walked
again, effortlessly we sensed where
& how to go—not through our eyes
but through our arms
and hips, our gait, noticing—
yet not noticing—the green shadows we
were moving through.
      In the middle
of the park, we stopped abruptly, both,
lifting our heads, testing the air like
ponies. Delirious lilacs? Lilies
of the valley? Apples?
      Turned as one.
Saw a Russian olive tree. Came to
stand under its silver green
branches. Fingerlings—musky
sweet flowers—fell around us
like willows, like swans.

      I looked up
at your face then: eyes, cheeks,
half-smile. Saw you whole. Your
wild golden corona shining
in an aura of yellow flowers, a galaxy
of stars.
      Jim, I said, an amnesiac
returning home. All the other faces
disappeared, floaters in this stream
of sun.

Midsummer in the Midwest

for Signe Birgitta Margareta Rønnmark Fowler

She had set the table with a blue and yellow cloth,
Because of Midsummer—she smiled, *the longest
day of the year* and the brim of her straw hat
bobbed with her excitement—
tiny wreaths of blue and yellow flowers
cradled each yellow candle, a folded yellow
napkin welcomed each china dinner plate.

Such finery for an American summer potluck—
cantelope boats, blue corn tortilla chips, greens
from the garden, chili with cumin, cayenne
and cloves. *When I was girl*, she continued, *my mother
served smoked salmon for Midsummer.
Cucumbers with dill, potatoes. That became our tradition.
And then for dessert the first
strawberries of the summer. How I had longed
for them the long winter months!*

*And then after dinner, while the grownups
sat and talked and drank, we went out
and picked seven kinds of wildflowers—
blue bachelor buttons, prestekrans, that's daisies—
that sort of thing. You made a bouquet
and put it under your pillow that night
and you would dream of your future beloved!*

That didn't work for me, she teased David—they'd
found each other in another country. She
rolled her eyes when she laughed. The curve
of her hat added a certain sense of play, mystery, even.
When she turned to talk to someone, you weren't sure
what expression would come back

to face you—the ironic grin, her brown eyes rolling
in exasperation, or her small frown of thoughtful nostalgia,
or her reflective gaze—
I haven't lost hope yet.

After dinner, she brought us strawberries
in small gilded bowls *from home.*
Then coffee. Dark chocolate—*for the magnesium
and anti-oxidants, of course.*

If you hadn't known her from before
you perhaps wouldn't realize her eyes
had not always been so hugely dark and beautiful—
you would perhaps not have noticed that her face
is somewhat thinner than before, and heart-shaped,
framing those eyes—

If you hadn't known her from before
you wouldn't think she was wearing a hat
because she'd lost most of her hair;
you'd think—*Look at that flirt! Look
at that playful woman!*

If you hadn't known her from before
you'd expect to see her bring out a straw basket
to match that hat, a basket for the young girl
scouting the woods for bachelor buttons
and *prestekrans,* her whole life
spread out before her.

A Day That Starts Out Gloomy Turns Out Brighter than Expected

after Raymond Carver

All day long the light
coming in the Venetian blinds was gray,
a decline from the 7 a.m. thunder-
bright sky. I hunched at my computer
determined to polish off the school year detritus—
for three days I'd tangled with schedules, email,
letters, manuscripts—so that summer
poems could begin, the ones hovering
like bronzy June bugs
in my periphery...

　　　　　　　　By the time I looked up
it was 2:30 p.m., time to drive over
to visit a friend with whom I had quarreled.
The sun came out as I pulled up to her house.
The bursting yellow iris made a meadow
of her yard. She took me on a tour.
Everything had been growing in my absence.
The poppies orange as shimmering taffeta,
the ginkgo tree full and shady, lavender
flutes, miniature day lilies—she forgot
their name. No matter, I probably wouldn't
remember anyway.

　　　　　　　　Inside, then, she offered
homemade chocolate cake. I noticed
her house as if visiting for the first time—
how the china plates circle above
the buffet—the bright purple poseys
on her Swedish Grandma's plate—
how the cat stands up on her hind legs to box

open the door—as if she were the original
Puss and Boots!—how my friend and I laugh
at the same things. How could I
have forgotten that?

              I can't recall
how we came to quarrel, exactly. The blow-up,
sure, I remember that. But the hurts
and slights—old habits and the stress of illness
that led up to it—they were more
difficult to track. I didn't try. *Why do it
if it makes you unhappy?* she said
about something else. The chocolate cake
did not make me unhappy. I totally enjoyed
her recitation of her recipe: *You take 2 squares
of unsweetened baking chocolate
and drop them in a cup of boiling water.
So you have to have a Pyrex measuring cup
that's bigger than the water
you need to measure. Then it melts…
The secret to the moisture
is the buttermilk…* And I enjoyed the fact
that when she said, *It's from Betty's mother,*
she didn't have to explain.
*Next time I'll I cut back on the sugar
even more.* Long-time friends—shorthand
for several lifetimes.

              When it was time
to go, she cut for me three fat peony buds.
Remembering how they are my favorite,
next to roses. At home, on my writing table,
they unfolded to a dark pink in the late
afternoon sun. The smell of summer, here again
for sure, slowly filled the room.

Still Point

I've seen a few splotches of bright yellow
in the black ash down the block
but today is the first real sign—
a red maple, a perfection
of fullness and symmetry
so perfect it looks like the trees
in *Aesop's Fables*—this maple tree
is changing colors, even though it's still July,
changing colors chromatically
from a pure dark green at the bottom
to yellow in the middle, then fire red
at her spiraling top, spiraling up
to blue.

At the sight of this beauty, my familiar
shudder of winter dread. But next
to this turn—a crab apple tree
drops her arms heavily, branches
full of ripe apples, each
apple boasting intensity
of color: crab apple green,
cinnamon red, red as Red Hots.

I love this crab apple tree, it reminds me of
grade school when we liked to
press down our colored pencils really really hard
to make all the colors bright & shiny—
remember the shiny dark leaves? I love
this tree, it reminds me of grade school when if
I'd say *I love the color red* the kids
would tease and say *If you love
it so much, why don't you marry it?*

I'm weak with the fullness of summer
weak with this beauty and yes!
I want to marry the whole world. Today,
such hesitation of the seasons—
summer in its fullness, winter dread,
both present at once—
which way to go?

I have to go home, I have to call
my sweetheart, I have to tell him *I love*
the crab apple trees and the red
maple tree, too. I have to
tell him *I think I'll die*
if we don't have sex before dark.

Windows: Fall Equinox

Did you balance an egg on end
at 12:27 p.m. today, the exact
time the sun left us for the south?
Some say the window of time—
30 seconds—is too short
to fool around with eggs. *How
do you know which 30 seconds
is the correct window?* My daughter,
at 12:27 p.m., at her computer screen,
balanced her checkbook.

I did neither. Went outside,
requisite ritual in times of change.
Turned on the garden hose, sprayed
the birdbath—smell of deep
deciduous woods. Power-sprayed
the kitchen windows. Storms down,
I'll see pinstriped nuthatches
diving at the feeder.

I stood in the yard a long while, seeing
no sun. Heard sobbing. A man's
hulking and heaving. Is it the weather?
Or something terrible he had not expected?
I nod to the hidden neighbor, *Yes,
we're in for it now.* I would talk to him
but which window opens to the room
that holds him is not clear.

At suppertime, the cardinals, as usual,
sit on the branch by our streaky window.
Watch us eating soba noodles. What
do they say, looking in? *Do they
mate for life? Which one
is the male? Will they stay here
through the winter snows, feed us
seeds until we lay our eggs again?*

Rose Quartz

I came to life millions of years ago, when an explosion of light broke a dark cliff into the pink side of the rainbow. For millennia I rested in that dark warm cave. One day, a young carver lifted me out of that undifferentiated pinkness, separated me from my ancestors and my progeny. She was bony and edgy, living in a house trailer and on the verge of bankruptcy at all times. Carving stones had not softened her. But when she worked, her hands showed the strength of thousands of ocean waves, her hands shaped curves from jagged edges. Her bony hands softened stone.

And so I became a clear thin circle, so thin that the light explodes into pinkness every morning it enters me again, as it did that moment of my birth.

My creator carried me and her other babies in a reed basket to the gathering on the prairie. There she placed me on a black silken cord. I waited in the sun, listening to the crickets and the crows. For several days, many admired me, but none chose me.

I knew the moment the quiet woman touched me that she needed to hold me against her heart. She had never thought of herself as lonely. But she stood alone. She had been sleeping in her tent, in the early morning coolness, and far into the afternoon. Now her hand closed on my smoothness—she was warm from the heat of the day. She held me all the way home where she put me in a dark drawer, taking my silky cord for another necklace. I do not understand these creatures.

I lost track of time. So I don't know when or why my life changed. One day she looped a leather sinew through my center—fine old leather, twisted and softened by a man's sweat. Now that cord holds me securely over her heart. I turn and shine as she walks through her day. I'm warmed by the blood warming her skin. Her fingers reach for me when she's nervous. How strange that, in the end—the light and dark, the cold and warm, the angled and smooth, the hard and soft—all arise from the same dark rainbow.

It's hard to know which one of us is opening the other, which one loves the other more.

IV

Winter Light

Winter Light

My mind is alert today.
from a morning meditation, December 10th

To be alert in the season of cold and dark, my mind
needs to be reminded of natural realities, like
the fact that even though bears go into hibernation,
they're only dozing. They're alert enough to give birth
without waking up. Imagine going home
from work today and not getting up
for the rest of the season. I heard last week
Florence Nightingale spent the last fifty years of her life
on her davenport. Too much sex in the war?
She was making a political statement, apparently,
but about what I didn't catch.

My mind drifted. It was picturing mother bears
dreaming the cold dark. Do they see the shiver
of the last green aspen leaves, the first snow
fluttering into the woods? Do they replay the music
of their cubs snuffling down grassy meadows
to the sandy beach? All the trees
have lost their leaves now, even the black oaks
are far-gone into winter sleep.

Remember these pictures. Otherwise
you might confuse normal desire
with a diagnosis, a mistaken analysis of cause
and effect. My friends, for instance, speak of severe
depression. One says, *I'm about to burst
from lethargy.* Another says, *I stand at the window
wishing I could get the energy
to do something. Anything.
Is it my marriage? Is it an old loss
I have not properly grieved? Am I running
away from intimacy?*

Take it from me, one who has also suffered.
Your mind does not want to be alert. Your mind's
desire, or lack of desire, has nothing to do
with your work, your childhood, your mother,
your marriage or lack of it, in short,
your spiritual life. Your mind is simply
tired of alertness—it wants to dream
in the dark.

So let it. Every morning fall into reverie
when you look out the window at the sleeping trees.
At noon, no matter how cold it is,
go outside, put out suet for the winter birds.
Picture the loons in the Gulf of Mexico
who had the sense to follow the light.

Midafternoon, light the lamp by the davenport.
Gather your books, afghan, hot milk and tea.
You may occupy the long evening ahead
practicing the dative in Finnish,
reading aloud the creation stories of the Ojibwe
and musing on many other intricacies
of the circumpolar
languages designed for this long winterdark.

When sleep comes over you, curl up
and dream of blueberries, sun
on the rocks, blue lakes so clear they're black.

This is the time to celebrate our kinship,
the one with the bears and the trees.

What To Do the First Morning the Sun Comes Back

Find a clean cloth for the kitchen table, the red and blue one
you made that cold winter in Montana. Spread out
your paper and books. Tune the radio to the jazz station.
Look at the bright orange safflowers you found last August—
how well they've held their color next to the black-spotted cat.

Make some egg coffee, in honor of all the people
above the Arctic Circle. Give thanks to the Sufis,
who figured out how to brew coffee
from the dark, bitter beans. Remark
on the joyfulness of your dishes: black and yellow stars.

Reminisce with your lover about the history of this kitchen
where, between bites of cashew stir fry,
you first kissed each other on the mouth. Now that you're hungry,
toast some leftover cornbread, spread it with real butter,
honey from bees that fed on basswood blossoms.

The window is frosted over, but the sun's casting an eye
over all the books. Open your Spanish book.
The season for sleeping is over.
The pots and pans: quiet now, let them be.

It will be a short day.
Sit in the kitchen as long as you can, reading and writing.
At sundown, rub a smidgen of butter
on the western windowsill
to ask the sun:
Come back again tomorrow.

I Fell in Love with the Tropics

after Raymond Carver

Because of the light
the broad expanses of light
over the hazy green mountains

Because it's dark at home in the winter

Because I love to wear purple and red and turquoise blue
in a country in love with black

Because of a first memory of small hands—
my fingers tracing curly vines
on Gramma's tooled leather purse

Because I'm a woman who lives in the reticent North

Desperadoes always
head South

Because of the light
the broad expanses of clear light
over the hazy blue mountains

Because Gramma went to Mexico to see Grandpa—
he worked on the railroad in the Depression—
and she was a taster, she just had to taste everything
and never got sick

Because a lover brought me here
and some folks still
ride horseback to the town square

Because my name *Lloyd*
means *gray* in Welsh—
it needs the balance
of magenta and fuchsia roses

Because all people
came from the topics, our bodies'
first home

.

Because I was housebound
in the North for too many years

Because of the light
the shifting expanses of light
falling across the courtyards

The light

Because Gramma talked to everybody
no matter where she was—her legacy to me

Because Guatemalans hug and pat each other
on the back, *Buen dia*
and women kiss me on the cheek

Because I talked with a Cakchiquel woman
and sketched Arabic arches and discovered
the åttebladros pattern on the blue and gold tiles
on the underside of the portico

Because Gramma loved the gardens of Lake Xochimilco
Take care what kind of beauty you love!
The second family legacy, beauty,
I'm finally able to choose

Because the Welsh fit in
wherever they go
and leave no trace of their path

Because it's dark at home in the winter

Because of the broad expanses of blue light
over the mountains

Because of the light
I already said that

The light

You Don't Have To

after reading "Wild Geese" by Mary Oliver

you don't have to be *green light go*
24/7 on time all the time touring
the organic macadamia nut farm
studying *501 Spanish Verbs*
all you have to do is poke around
walk the cobblestone streets
you were born pokey you know that
you're good at being pokey on time
Guatemalan time and it's not
because your mother
read you *The Pokey Little Puppy*
that Golden Book about
the puppy always late to dinner
don't blame that puppy
don't blame your mother either
when you're being pokey time stops
remember how your watch stopped
the day you got here? and the next day
your clock? remember how you
sat on the sofa reading a novel
in Dayton's Furniture Department
when you were supposed to
meet your mother by the big clock?
when you're being pokey pictures
come to you   sensations from this world
and the other poplar leaves on a stream
in Montana suddenly they make a pattern
out of your thirst for quinine water
a volcano named Agua
the four channels of the Bitterroot River
where you buried your cat the fierce one
the one who thought she was a dog

the one who let your daughter
put her in the baby stroller like a doll
your girl's arms stretching
up to the handles   now this
gray and white cat on the portico
where you sit writing   your fountain pen
from seventh grade with its hungry belly
its snout slurping noisily
from its bottle of black ink
the dark woman with strong teeth
chewing a pig's bladder
to give the Virgin's face
a pearly glow church bells
dinning like Chinese gongs
the gold sun on the altar
bursting out like the breast plates
of the Sami women   sola!
mother of us all! these impossible purple
roses on Irma's white pique dress
her long black hair held back
by a scrunchy   her hands
patting out corn & lime tortillas
like her mothers for a thousand years—
this is what you've been thirsting for
the orange blossoms
in the courtyard this morning
heady delicate sweet
three ripe oranges
just out of reach

Santa Clara Convent, Antigua, Guatemala

They were girls, really,
    the nuns who walked up
        this spiral staircase,
           the steps so shallow and narrow
  I don't dare step up
more than two. Ancient earthquakes
    swept the upper stairs
        and roof away—
           steps stopping
                at the second turn mid-air—
           three hundred years
        of rain and wind
    have worn down the steps
that stay, bricks morphing
    back to sand, moss
        softening every squared corner
           to a curve—
        and yet I still see the smallness
    of their feet, the fold
in their ankles as they
    ascend—girls barely out
        of childhood, sent from
           Spain and Mexico, never
        to see their mothers again.

And what lifted their spirits
    in their spiral flight? The blueness
        of this mountain air,
    the golden butterfly,
the cypress tree?

¿Qué Es?

for P.K.P.

Here I am in your beloved tropics, holding up a fat blue stick
and asking Don Rodrigo *¿Qué es?* What is it?
He rattles off a stream of talk and when I look dumbfounded,
he fishes one of my dirty socks out of my laundry pail,
lays it out flat on the left side of the *pila*—
concrete angled like a washboard but permanent,
so it doesn't slip when you scrub—and arranges the sock flat
in its perfect sockness: a Christmas cookie.

Then he takes the blue stick and holds it up for my attention.
El creyón. He articulates loudly to the dumb foreigner.
I dutifully answer. *El creyón.* Nodding approval, he
turns *el creyón* on its side and rubs it down the sock—
from tip to toe—narrating in Spanish non-stop.
Picks up the sock, rubs it against the bumps.
Turns it over. Repeats. Turns it
inside out. Pats it into cookie shape. Repeats the scrub.
Other side, same story. What does it mean, he must
be thinking, that these *gringas*
bring such soiled clothes to my laundry? Finally,
he dips a small bowl into the middle tub of the *pila:*
clean water. He rinses the sock, wrings it hard
and sets it on the edge. *¡Bien!*

I take this to mean I should do my laundry
by his methods, not my lazy soak-and-rinse. And so I scrub
and listen to his salsa gospel playing
from the radio on the automatic washer next to me.
The patio is lined with old busted-up appliances: each one
covered with an embroidered cloth: on one,
Don Rodrigo's dishes and three enameled pans; on another
a small gas stove, and by the door:
one old fedora, one cowboy hat, crisp black felt.

Don Rodrigo's gestures bring your stories back to life,
as though you were right here talking: *Castro*, you said,
Castro said he never trusted a man who didn't cook
his own food, wash his own socks. And then you said,
you said you could hardly wait to retire, to wash your own
socks; you could hardly wait to throw away your
Western suits, spend the rest of your life
by the Indian Ocean, reading and writing.

Don Rodrigo would rank high on your list of
heroes but what would you say today, the day that CNN
shows us Castro in a Western suit greeting
the white-skirted man from Rome? Does it mean
Castro has stopped washing his own socks? Or simply
that his people are hungry and he's doing what he can?
Or maybe that was just one of your stories. *¿Cuál es?*

What does it mean that you are not here in the tropics
to amuse me? So many of us loved your stories.
You'd like the jacket I found in the market
yesterday, indigo. You'd like the shopping in the courtyards
out of the sun. What does it mean that I am here
living out the rest of my life
reading and writing, picking up *el creyón*,
learning how Castro
may have once washed his socks?

Indigo

The first time I went to Guatemala they told us *Don't drink the water* and *Don't buy the first thing you see* but the first day I saw this indigo jacket and I bought it in spite of the warning, and I don't know why I fell in love with it at first sight, but Carol loved it too and said *Go ahead and get it*, and so I did, the beautiful indigo with random pale stripes—not much of a pattern, really, but on the back there were two bands of embroidery making a cross: bursts of purple and red and cobalt, and I liked the weight on my shoulders, and I liked the embroidery that glowed like jewels and the cross reminded me of my favorite quote of Black Elk, the one about the road of difficulties, and the vertical line up my back reminded me of all my chakras, activated, and the horizontal cross across my shoulders reminded me to feel my own strength, you know, open up and not be hunched over like the depressed person I often believe I am. And every time I wore my jacket I wished I knew who had made the cloth—I knew it was hand woven, of course, even though it had been fashioned into a Western style jacket, for foreigners, but I wished I knew the village it came from, I wished I knew the woman who made it.

Two years later, back in Guatemala, some of us went farther up into the mountains for the market day at the village of Santa Maria de Jesus, and as I got out of the van I felt a rush come over me: all the women in the market were wearing skirts of indigo cloth, the same pattern as my jacket. Women in indigo walking with jugs of water on their heads. Women in indigo watching over baskets of food for sale: baskets of avocados, peppers, eggs, tomatoes, a pile of cut sugarcane by a truck. Women in indigo holding babies and cooking tortillas on old tin pans over open fires. Women in indigo sitting on woven mats, working and tending to their children, barefoot. But there was only one woman selling meat: pieces of armadillo roasted with chilis and pumpkin seeds, flavored like pepian, a favorite dish. The head of the armadillo was still whole, the eyes looking up at me as sweetly as a pet puppy. Five or six bony dogs gathered around her, sniffing, looking for an in. She kept shooing them away and laughed and taught us the Cakchiquel word for dog, *se-eh*. I practiced, not getting the last consonant correct, it was kind of a lilting at the back of the throat, and I knew I couldn't quite get it right but she said I did great, in Spanish, no English, and all the kids wanted me to say it again and so I did and I told them I was excited to learn my first Cakchiquel word and I would practice it when I went home but even all their praise could not convince me to taste the roasted armadillo. I was freaked out that this was the only meat they had. I hoped my shock didn't show. No running water, no shoes, no Band-aids for their kids' cuts and scrapes. So many *no's*. No broccoli or cauliflower for sale from the dark green fields—it all goes to export. No roses for sale, they all go to Northerners, hungry for color. No coffee for sale—nothing to drink but coconut. Pale yellow, surprisingly cool, juice coming out of a rough shell.

And how could I tell her, this woman who taught me to say my first word of Cakchiquel, *se-eh*, that I would remember her when I went back home? How could I tell her that when I got home and put on my indigo jacket from Santa Maria de Jesus that I would decide that *she* was the one who wove the indigo cloth, that she was the one who sewed the bands of reds and purples, the woman in indigo shooing the dogs and laughing, the woman in indigo sitting in the middle of the market with her kids, the woman joking with these foreigners, all of us who were in awe of her and her friends, who, in the chaos of hunger and poverty, bring forth this beauty with their hands.

San Antonio Agua Calientes

And then we rode in the back of the pickup to go up to the village to see Zoila Garcia to learn the real way to make tortillas and pepian—with three kinds of peppers and pumpkin seeds and chicken and garlic and onion—and the dirt road was rutted, the mountainsides steep, burn/slash checkerboards in gorgeous shades of green just like the guidebook book said—but what the guidebook didn't say was how dusty it was out in the countryside—all that dust thrown up by the pick up mixed with the exhaust from the trucks—mixed with the stirred up grit from the volcano—mixed with the smoke from the wood fires, that friendly smell of childhood now coming at us in a new presentation—and the mist fingering down from the mountain pass farther up moistened and coated everything together even though the sun was so hot and the wind and we were tasting grit and my hair got thick (and had "body") and the little kids that jumped on the back fender of the pickup with the scraped up faces were grimy too and we were grimy even though we'd had some kind of shower that morning and worried there wouldn't be any hot water when we got back (being the tourists that we were) but it was fabulous anyway with the sun and the green and the wind—

And as we got higher and past the hot springs—*agua calientes*—the road got more rutted and I held onto the little kids on the back bumper so they wouldn't fall off and we started to see people walking down past us from higher up in the mountains: one old woman had a load of firewood so huge it was half as big as she was and it was all wrapped neatly on her head with red & purple cloth, the sticks sawed in equal lengths and *How many years has she been doing this? Walking into the forest barefoot?* and next came a couple of women, each holding a couple of small sticks in one hand, *Well, how much could that cook?* and *Why didn't they have time to find more?* and at the turn by the store, a man grinning wildly walked by with a huge branch—a real find—still covered with moss and fungus the length of most of the houses, a forest in itself almost, and *There goes the rain forest* and as we slowed down at Zoila's fence, a really old woman came walking slowly bent over with a bundle on her head, slowing down to stare friendily at this pickup of *gringas* her bare feet spread wide from years of walking up and down this mountain,

Diego Rivera didn't exaggerate when he painted big feet... your feet would spread too if you had to work this hard for a fire—

And later, back in town, with the smell of smoke comforting my clothes and hair—not even wanting to wash out that childhood safety—I read in the newspaper: *A man, his wife, and their seven-year old daughter were killed by private security guards for cutting wood illegally on a finca near Antigua. The crime came to light Thursday after the bodies of the three were found in the village of San Bartolome Becerra Antigua Guatemala.* That would be the village over, next to the one we drove to in the pickup, the rutted road much like any other, the road to San Antonio Agua Calientes, where people risk their lives to roast some peppers, fry some tortillas, heat up a pot of beans.

How to Be Middle Class

In Guatemala
Have a house, a concrete block house with a corrugated tin roof
Have a refrigerator, a little black and white TV
and a husband with a job and a motorscooter
You'll be middle class even if
you have to cook over a woodstove
use a green garden hose outside for water
boil the water for cooking

When a bus shows up to go to town, jump on!
You never know when the next one will come

In Norway
Everybody already has a house, a car, healthcare
five weeks vacation and a cabin in the mountains,
so what you have to have
to be middle class is
the education to know
how to move around
the freedom to choose what you want to do

When it's time to go to work, walk to the corner, hop a streetcar, a bus—
everybody does it
even the blondes in saris and high heels

In the United States
Have a job that makes enough money to get you a big house
a big car, a big garage, a big house far away from people who take the bus
Don't date anybody without healthcare
Be able to say *I have no idea where to catch a bus to the Mall*
Do not have anywhere in your head the knowledge that the bus driver calls
out *CUB TARGET RAINBOW* instead of street names
for all the folks who take the bus to get their groceries

When it's time to go to work, hop in your car
do your fast drive-by
past all the places where the poor people live
all the mysterious places
the buses go

sections to be added by readers....

A Dozen Reasons to Give Up Haggling over the Price of Weavings

1   for the weaver herself who takes the bus to market at 4 a.m.
1.5   for the buck and a half she brings home each day
2   for the discount rate *para dos* she offers too readily
3   for the 3 languages she speaks, working on the 4th
4   for her babies born after the war
         one for the cousin killed in the highlands
         one for the uncle in Minnesota
         two for the brother and sister hiding in Mexico
5   for the age she started to weave
6   for her favorite colors: canario, rojo, verde, morado, indigo y cafe
7   for the quetzal/dollar exchange
8   for the animals who dance in her cloth:
         cat, quetzal, monarch, hummingbird, deer
         squirrel eating chamomile, chick, and dove
9   for the tortillas in her apron pocket
10   for ten fingers she says she's lucky to have
11   for the family she has to feed
12   for the men, the dozens of unmarked graves

Another View of Culture: She Explains Why She Loves Disney Cartoons

and one day we heard a sound and it was boom boom
schh schh schh and i thought it was the fireworks
and i said to my mother *whose birthday today?*
and she said *get under the bed* and bullets
were coming in our house *schh schh schhhh*
and one day when i walked to school
i saw three naked bodies around the flagpole
lying on the ground
but i couldn't read the blood
the words the guerrillas had written on the bodies
and one day the army roared up in their trucks
and grabbed boys off the street
threw them up in the back of the truck
that's what they call *recruiting*
some of them my cousins
and one day there were many people in the graveyard
it was the Days of the Dead and *schh schh schhh*
the helicopters came out of the sky
and they were shooting at all the people
down on the ground with their golden flowers
and we could hear the noise *schh schh schh*
and one day my mother
said *you cannot go outside to play anymore*
the cartoons were so funny *BEEP BEEP*
what do you call him in English?
he was my favorite but the other ones too
the Duck Family and Mickey
and one day my mother and father sent me
to another place to keep me safe
even though i would be far away
from them   far away from home.

a found/heard poem from someone who asks to be anonymous

Poem on the Occasion of the Festival of the Immaculate Conception, Antigua, Guatemala, & the Confirmation of John Ashcroft as Attorney General of the U.S., 2001

From behind the float, we can see Mary's long curly hair, thick & dark as that of most of the women walking. The two angels kneeling beside her also have thick hair, sturdy wings. Because they're kneeling, we can see the soles of their feet, smooth & bare, like the woman walking next to me, walking barefoot. This old woman is not watching her step like us *gringas*, she's not having any trouble walking these rough cobblestones, even though she's bent over from age & work. She moves with smooth certainty, busy greeting the people who have come out of their houses to see the procession. She pays no mind to the cobblestones, the puddles, the sharp edges of debris—nor to the hundreds of calla lilies spread extravagantly on the cobblestones for Mary, & so for all the women walking with her—the women in magenta satin dresses (like Mary on the float) the women in black leather jackets holding their mothers by the arm, mothers in shawls, the women from villages in their hand-woven clothing, & the little girls: the little girl right here on the sidewalk curled up in her pink net Sunday dress, barefoot, eating McDonald's French fries—

& suppose you were here today, Mr. New Attorney General, in your crispy white shirt, your shiny shoes, your black & white legal certainties—would you take off your shoes for Mary? Would you kneel to Maria Madre de Dios? Would you spread red rose petals across the stones in honor of both conception & its contra? How will you honor every living woman's immaculate life?

In the Name of the Daughter

at a hotel built on the ruins of a Dominican monastery

Where the monks once walked, I, female, heretic, walk.
I'm the naughty Goldilocks, tasting their soup,
admiring the gilded statues at every turn,
swimming in the shaded pool, sleeping in their beds—
cotton sheets softer than any I've known before.
When I pass a painting of a dead Dominican,
I say a prayer of thanks. *This rest
restoreth my soul.* My pleasure doubled
by the sense of trespass.

The thick walls hold in the night's coolness
all day. They buffer the noise of trucks
on cobblestones, birthday firecrackers, shouts.
In the inner gardens, calla lilies spray up
out of fountains. Birds of paradise
fly from stone urns. The original shape of the stone
arches that fell away in the earthquakes
are now re-imagined with trellised roses,
and at night, tiny white lights make their own
arching Milky Ways. The lights remind
me of the grade school blackboard, how we
carefully chalked in each one of
the Big Dipper's seven stars.

This last night, alone, I walk out
into the garden. The stars are close to Earth.
But I cannot find the Big Dipper anywhere.
Only Orion, straight overhead.
The sparkling belt of the hunter, unmistakable.
Goldilocks as Orion, there's a thought.
After my life as Demeter, I've turned into
Orion, Diana, Goldilocks—my feet,

called to travel, not knowing the purpose
or the goal. It comes easily, this traveling,
as long as I stay grounded in the sky.

Suddenly it is urgent for me to call my sweetheart
on the hotel phone to tell him the Big Dipper
is missing. We talk through the snowy static
where North is—I tell him, too, that the sheets
are starry soft, that he should be sleeping in my bed.
I tell him it's about time the Dominicans admitted
Goldilocks to their care—and I tell him it's time
for me to pack my bags. *I'm on my way home,*
tomorrow, soon.

V

Northern Sun

Natt og Dag: Return to Norway after 25 Years

I wanted to know the names of things,
words I'd forgotten, words I'd never learned
the first time: the name of the violet,
for instance, snuggling in the crack
of the mossy boulder by the cabin.
A sunny gold face with a purple forehead,
purple hair.
        The two women disagreed
about its name. Eva said, *Its name is Dag*
og Natt, that's Day and Night. She should know,
she said, she'd been picking them ever since
she was a girl. The other, Mette, said, *Oh, no,*
most definitely not. Its name is Natt
og Dag, because the night
is the mother of the day. Not the other way
around.
        They went back and forth.
Each stood her ground. At first I favored Eva's
childhood memory, being who I am. Impressed
that she sported fuchsia toenails—the exact match
to her shiny rain suit. And that she walked
barefoot in the rain—
all tan and fuchsia!
        But in the end
I had to go with Mette's naming,
being who I am. Because it pleased me.
Comforted me, even. Because I kept on
saying her words whenever I saw a dark purple
violet with a golden face... *Natt og Dag.*
Natt og Dag. Fordi natten
er dagens mor.
        Because the night is
the mother of the day.

White Nights: Another Woman of the North Talking

These are magical nights, these white nights
after the long winter sleep when nobody
wants to sleep. Look how we keep sitting
and talking, long after the barbecue has died down—
the cousins, the grandkids, the hired man
who came to help put up the hay—
everyone awake! Look at the purple lupine!
The haze over the valley!
Who can bear to go in the house?

Have you heard about the fairy tale:
The Boy Who Fell into the Hedge?
He fell in love with the sweet white blossoms
under the window of the girl he was courting.
What was it he fell in love with? The fragrance
the blossoms wrapped around him? The way the
pale petals reflected the sun at midnight, or
their silky touch, the insides of
ocean shells? Whatever
it was, he surrendered—turned
himself into blossoms.

*What can bring him back? What can break
the spell?* Maybe he didn't want
to come back. Maybe he loved summer.
Maybe he didn't want to have to
be with a girl or maybe, just maybe, the girl
dove into the flowering hedge with him.

Did that happen long ago or only last week?
Nobody knows. If you go to sleep now, you
can wake up at 3 a.m. and see a pink sky,
a neon pink sun. There is so much sun
all night, we even have silver mesh

curtains, soft screens, to pull across the windows...

It might be cloudy at 7 a.m.
but the light will fill your bed.
You'll sense that a whole world has been going on
since you nodded off. People will be talking in the kitchen
making coffee. *Did they go to bed*
at all? you will wonder.

One thing you can know for sure.
It will be an eternity until the sun disappears
behind the mountains. It will be
an eternity until the snow
fills your window
instead of this sweet blossoming hedge.

Summer Dinner Party in Oslo:
Margery Tells a Story of Her Ancestors

Three sisters escaped from the Ukraine with nothing—
they were Jews who got out before the pogroms.
Came to Brooklyn, worked in the garment district
like so many others. Their apartment had no
electricity—for light they had gas sconces
on the walls. Now, picture this, to turn on the light
they had to put a quarter in the gas meter
which was very high up on the wall. Tiny—
they were tiny people, these Ukrainian women.

Now, the man next door was from Sicily—
taller than they were. So they asked him
every night to help them out—because
he could reach, you know. So he had three
young women to pick from. But maybe
it wasn't the man who did the choosing.
Maybe one of the sisters had her eye
on him, because of course
she could've used a footstool to stand on
to put the quarter in. They weren't that poor!

So that was that love story.
He had a lot of work as a plasterer,
twirled fancy roses on the moldings,
the corners of the ceilings. Like cake.
That all came to an end in 1929.
Then he stayed home. Did the family cooking.
A gallon of olive oil on the stove. For salad,
one finger halfover the top of the wine bottle, wine
gone to vinegar, of course. A splash. Taught
his daughter to cook. That was my mother.

That's why I know my way
around the kitchen, how my children came to
know a good salad when they taste it. But how
I got Norwegian citizens for children, that's
a story for another night—tonight
I bring you not only potato salad but also
a jar of celery seeds fresh from back
across the Atlantic—and a hand-written copy
of my recipe. American.

We Didn't Have the Words Then

for Turid

But now that we do, we cover the distance
of thirty-eight years in a few hours.

*Manic-depressive. Incest. Class. The capacity
to make choices.* Then what happens? Yoga

on the sunny deck. Talk of less important mysteries.
What is the price of deck furniture

when you want to follow the sun all day and don't
want to have to keep moving your chair?

Why do men in the Shetland pubs scowl at Norwegians?
Do rowan trees grow in the States? Do I look like a matron?

Now it's time to check the leaves on the broken branch of
the cherry tree we duct-taped last night. And now

there's a radio program, an actor reading from a book,
a book we took to heart, strangely enough, each from our own side

of the Atlantic: *You must never believe that you know anything,
You must never believe that anyone cares about you.*

The childhoods we have now survived.
Coffee with strong cream. Blue clouds. Islands in the fjord.

Even a few cigarettes. Smoke and talk of the winter darkness.
Sundown in the Caribbean. *Vi skulle jo få glede av livet.*

By the end of the afternoon, the laundry basket is empty—
a dozen of Rolv's dress shirts, one embroidered blouse,

five blouses for work, matron slacks—huge fuchsia zinnias—
and five woven tablecloths

hang smooth and fresh, the smell of ironing
blending with the sweet hydrangeas growing thick on the stone wall.

Lying Down in Public Places

Last summer I took to walking to the park after work, stretched out on the picnic table. Pressed my lower back flat. Felt the sun on my face, smelled juniper, dust, sweat. Off-loaded every damn twitch from the day's work. Off-loaded memories, spasms, seizures, fears, petty worries, tics... Enough of a list, you get the idea.

This continued when I traveled. In Wales I suddenly had to go down at the foot of a Celtic cross 600 years old. That was some real serious off-loading. Up at the writers' retreat on the North Shore I found a perfect flat rock with a shelf for my legs, sort of like a chair tipped backwards. *Ah, Pre-Cambrian shield* is what I would say as I tilted back. Great off-loading there too. A great shift from the work indoors, cramped over the dark desk.

Lying down works in more mundane places: a park bench, a dock, a fallen tree in a park (that would be a log), a bench in a museum. Lying on your side, backpack for a pillow, the lower back lets loose, off-loading of the mind begins. The magnetic pull of the earth pulls it free. The people around me gossip, confide, carry on. As if I can't hear them. They must think I'm homeless, that is, hard of hearing? Some think I'm sleeping, I suppose, or stalling, or procrastinating, or wasting time. Dreamers, they may say, lying down when they could be up, making something of their lives. If you didn't sleep so much, you wouldn't sleep so much.

But it doesn't matter what they say, as I said, I have a task to do. All the concerns of humanity wash over me. Sometimes I take in a phrase for a poem, but mostly, you know, as I said before, I'm off-loading. Just yesterday when I was lying down on a log rubbing a tight back muscle on a strong knot of bark (almost as good as a massage), a little girl a few feet away announced, *Mother, I can't stand another minute in this sun, I want to go home now.* This girl has to be in a poem, drama queen in training, and it might as well be this poem. When I was a little girl I did not know how to announce such needs to the world.

Now I'm playing catch up with my sudden tip and fold. My friends have gotten used to it. They take my habit as a photo op. Jim snapped me at the cross, Barb on the gnarled log. Mari Elena caught my stretch on the angled roof of the Posado San Sebastian. Imagine my surprise last week when I opened the newsletter from the writers' retreat and saw a picture of an otter playing in the lake and read the caption, *Here's the otter that woke Roseann up when she was taking her nap.*

The Color of Hills and Water

It's said that ancient Celtic warriors, women and men, went into battle naked and covered their bodies with blue paint, as though they were savages. What should be added to this story is that this paint, which they made from the woad plant, contained antiseptic properties that protected them in battle.

And you can't tell the difference between blue and green when you're driving down to the sea, especially that windy one-lane road coming down to Solva and you say the only expression you know in Welsh: *tylwyth teg, tylwyth teg*, it's a song all to itself and you believe it, for you've traveled through the tree tunnels and stood under the dark hawthorn trees with their sudden cloud of faery bloom, and you can't tell the difference between blue and green when you're squinting sea side and the wind blasts your bleak city thoughts out of your brain and the water dances up to throw *aqua blue* across your field of vision, turquoise and forest green, even, too, and it's no surprise that old Welsh has a word for a color that means both blue and green: *glas, the color of hills and water*, it says in my word-book, and when you're walking along the hedgerows from your car to the sea you sense all that *glas* humming hot around you and you know it's the color of life, the color from which the fuchsia foxgloves burst and you keep walking and when you walk into the deep wooded garden you come upon blue poppies, yes! you're not even stoned and the poppies are shimmering blue, brindled with sun and green, and you know for a fact that *glas* should become an English expression, too, and you say it out loud, *glas*, your second word in Welsh, and only then do you see the blue warriors skating through the deep green woods, the blue warriors, leaf-splashed, sun-brindled—all our city wounds cured by blue.

All I Knew about Wales Was That Grandpa Loved Ponies

for my Welsh grandpa, Guy Leslie Lloyd, 1890-1955

I didn't know the high cliffs above the Irish Sea plunged—
purple gray granite—straight down into the sheer
rocks and skerries   I didn't know that the cliffs
would be covered with gorse and purple heather
all of it growing up and growing down
and that tiny red lilies
would wave over St. Non's Spring

> All I knew about Wales was that Grandpa loved
> ponies   the small ponies that worked the coal mines
> and peat bogs   the ponies even a child could ride

I didn't know that the paths along the cliffs
wandered through open meadows and deep tunnels
of hedge   the hedge forming arches
like those in fairy tales I didn't know that I would
look up from the narrow path to see a crowd
of white cows pressing against the fence—right above us
on a cliff's edge   our Welsh friend saluting
Hello   Ladies

> All I knew about Wales was that Grandpa loved
> ponies and his cows   the black Angus cows
> obisidian shiny in the sun

I didn't know so many fairy tales would
appear as I walked the cliffs—Sleeping Beauty
guarded by thorny hedges   Silkies in the silver foam
the Wise Old Crone in the hawthorn   Healthcliff waving his arms
wailing in the wind   I didn't know I would feel content
in rain-soaked clothes   walking with my beloved
along these cliffs   I didn't know I would be so glad

that he is the man I traveled with to Wales
not one of those crazy Heathcliffs
I loved *once upon a time*

        All I knew about Wales was that Grandpa loved his
        ponies and his cows and my gramma—
        Gramma who told me *I had a romance once*

I didn't know I'd find such delight
finding fat blackberries along the thorny path
I didn't know that I would gently touch the darkest one
to see if it were ripe enough to fall
into my hand—so I could put it in my lover's mouth
I didn't know I'd feel at ease walking down
to the Caerfai beach—*seaside*—they say over here
walking into the sea letting my feet sink
deep into the white sand icy cold water rushing my knees
up my legs—nobody but little kids
swimming

        All I knew about Wales was that Grandpa loved ponies
        that he gave his kids a circus pony to ride
        on their inland farm   far from the Irish Sea

I didn't know I would crave the sea salt wind
that I'd want to walk to St. Non's Spring
again and again for her constancy of sounds welling up
from deep inside the earth   I didn't know I'd dream
the waiter at our nightly restaurant
grabbing the piles of fried fishes on our plates
and throwing them back into the sea—
where, wildly thrashing, they replenish
the oceans with life

        All I knew about Wales was that Grandpa loved ponies
        that his parents got married on horseback
        his mother six months pregnant carrying him
        already on her wedding day

I didn't know that I would come to Wales
during the last full eclipse of the millennium
that I would sit by St. Non's Spring
the bubbling sound of water a comfort
during that fearful momentary lull—I didn't know
that Virginia Woolf wrote about an eclipse
in 1927... *the cold increased as the light went down...*
and so I write this in her memory and in the memory of
all my lost kin the Lloyds on whose ground I finally walked—
for all of us who need the blessings of water
not a lonely watery death—

           All I knew about Wales was that Grandpa loved his ponies
           that he promised to buy me a pony when I turned 12
           but didn't live that long

I didn't know that my grandpa would be with me
in Wales especially with me the last day when I walked
up the cliffs from the sea in my sandy feet
when Welsh ponies strolled over nibbled my fingers
tossed their blond manes over to one side
turned their necks for a good scratch

I didn't know that I would discover then
that I had come around full circle
learning how to make the North
my home.

The Woman They Found in Siberia

after reading Good Heart *by Deborah Keenan*

the woman they found in siberia last year,
like the man in the alps, has been dead a long time.

they're counting millennia,
not centuries, when they say *a long time.*

yet she is still wearing her silk dress
and her headdress, a tree with birds.

they don't say what color the dress is
or the names of the birds

but would i like that kind of burial?
of course. not even knowing which birds.

that's the answer, of course, why else
would i have brought it up? now in this age

of poets who interrupt long-winded
poems with ironic questions and short answers—

do you think i can get the hang of that
before i go? h'mmm. unlikely, rambling one.

get the longest silk winding sheet for me,
my wind-swept poems. make sure it's got blue in it

and gold. just kidding, i've
made other plans for my post-life condition.

ashes in our lakeshore property,
the local graveyard that has a pond.

but the headdress is so appealing.
and the idea of my own personal tree of life.

with my birds: willing. the red-winged
blackbirds in the montana marshes.

the cedar wax-wings feasting noisily on orange
berries of the mountain ash after my brother died,

calling me back to life. the elusive cardinals
who answer my calls.

the tail-waggers, too, the finches. the slow-
motion herons. the eagles. the loons.

and the crows. always the crows. all
the songs i have claimed. all the songs

that have claimed me.

End Notes

She Said

The Sami believe *The sun is the mother of all living things.*
The Japanese have an ancient myth about women's work bringing back the sun.
All the names of wildflowers in this poem are the Norwegian names, which I
translated.

The Midsummer Ghazals

These poems came from the practice one summer of writing a ghazal each day,
based on the images and events of that day, inspired by Adrienne Rich's "The
Blue Ghazals." I wrote these during a time of transition in my work and family
life.

My ghazals, as they evolved, are structured with the following elements of the
traditional form from Iran/Persia, including: a minimum of five couplets; each
couplet an intact unit with no enjambment to the next couplet; each couplet
free to claim its own tone (varying from serious, flippant, casual, philosophical,
humorous); and the use of one's own name in the last couplet. In this way, the
effect of the ghazal is like that of a mosaic. I didn't use the rhyme scheme of the
traditional ghazal because *English is a rhyme-poor language*, a statement often
repeated by one of my first teachers, Richard Hugo. In place of the rhyming pat-
tern of the traditional form, I looked for other ways to bring a sense of repeti-
tion and containment into the poems: each ghazal contains images from a
dream from the night before; each ghazal also seeks to find a place for the words
lavender, *gold*, and *thunder*.

Specific references in the ghazals:

All the way to heaven… is a quote from St. Catherine of Sienna.

Zi Ye is a Chinese poet, female, who wrote poems more than 2000 years ago.
Thanks to Jane Hirshfield for bringing her to American readers.

*If they ask, what is the sign of the one who sent you, answer/It is a movement and a
rest.* is a quote from a Gnostic liturgy, unpublished.

Resorting to Metaphor

the musical insistence of their wings… is a quote from the poem "On the Gift of The Birds of America by John James Audubon," *Outside History*, by Eavan Boland.

Mørketiden: The Dark Time

This poem is based on part of an old Scandinavian creation myth. The Norwegian term *Mørketiden* means literally *The Dark Time*. In Norway it is used to describe the winter period when people in the far North cannot see the sun.

Recollect

The poem is dedicated to Julie Dash, the film-maker, creator of *Daughters of the Dust*; the words *recollect, remember, recall* are a litany throughout the film, a call to African-American people to carry their own ancestral heritage with them, wherever they go. My poem is based on my own ancestral images from the North; it is not anthropologically accurate.

tyttebær is the Norwegian word for mountain cranberries.

when your limbs are scattered is an quote from Isaiah, not, as someone asked, a reference to an obscure Aztec ritual.

Field Trip: Kids from the Treatment Center Visit the Art Institute

Jade carvers worked long at their craft: the museum placard informs us that jade must be *polished until luminous*. How many years that takes they do not say, but jade is one of the hardest stones to polish. This piece is on display at the Minneapolis Institute of Arts, Minneapolis, Minnesota.

Sorrow Comes in Spades

U.S. Senator Paul Wellstone and his wife Sheila recognized the connection between domestic violence and other violence. The federal law, which was passed under their leadership, generally known as the Violence Against Women Act, prohibits, among other things, those persons under a restraining order for domestic violence from possessing a firearm. It is because of the law that the man alleged to be the sniper in the Washington, D.C., area, 2002, could be held and detained until other evidence was gathered.

The word *spade* and the last line come from John Caddy's poem "EarthJournal Entry 10.25.2002. "

EarthJournal Entry 10.25.2002

Earthworms push deeper now, squeeze
through fissures in the soil, now
toads with squeezed eyes
spade down with hind clawed legs
with old cold-blood strength, then
with front legs pull the loose soil up,
pack it tight above their heads
to evade the crystals
frost is reaching down,
crystal filaments like
dendrites growing down
with a message burned in ice.

Toads slumber, but ice is a wakeup call. In a harsh northern winter they will move five feet down. What a simple, excellent strategy, if you have the strength and don't mind digging when you're half asleep.
—John Caddy

Falling Means You Have the Chance to Learn to Walk Again

House finches have small gray bodies with reddish shading moving down their heads and chests.

In the Season of Chanterelles

This form of this poem is the ghazal; see notes on "The Midsummer Ghazals." The Rumi quote in line 10 is from Rumi's poem #1616.

Look for huge oaks with long, sparse grass underneath... is a quote from poet and forager Ilze Mueller.

Through patience the mulberry leaf turns to satin is a Turkish proverb. I wrote the poem in July 1998. Shortly afterwards, in the fall, an elder in our congregation, Fern Smith, died of a heart attack. Fern had spent eight years teaching in Turkey. Her books were given to the congregation and in one I discovered the proverb about the mulberries. It is a gift to me and to this poem from Fern.

Walking Along the River Bluff, We Glimpse a Whir of Red Wings in the Brush

This poem emerged after reading Rumi's poem #1246.

Blind-Sided

This poem was also inspired by Rumi's poem #1246.

Midsummer in the Midwest

In Scandinavia the summer solstice is celebrated on June 23. The first Christians moved the solstice from the 21st to the 23rd and called it St. John's Day (in Norway, *Sankt Hans*) but it retains its original solstice joy, the longest day of the year. It is still one of the primary celebrations of the year, with bonfires, barbecues on the beach, and boats decorated with wreaths and flags.

What to Do the First Morning the Sun Comes Back

coffee is a reference to the history of this drink. In Persia/Turkey, coffee beans were originally ground up with rancid butter and used for travel gorp along the silk road and other long overland routes: the Sufis figured out how to turn the beans to a drink for their all-night dancing and singing adventures.

pots and pans refers to an ancient custom in the British Isles; people banged on pots and pans the night of the solstice, making a big racket, to bring the sun back.

butter on the windowsill refers to an custom which is still observed in some parts of northern Norway.

I Fell in Love with the Tropics

Åttebladros means *eight-petalled rose* in Norwegian; it is an ancient Scandinavian design.

You Don't Have To

The religious painters in Central America used a substance found in the pig's bladder and combined it with gold foil to make a paint for the "skin color" of the wooden statues. This was called *encarnada*. Local people were recruited for the task of chewing pig's bladders to release the substance.

Indigo

You have set the powers of the four quarters to cross each other. The good road and the road of difficulties you have made to cross; and where they cross, the place is holy.
The quote from Black Elk is from *Black Elk Speaks: Being the Life Story of a Holy Man of the Oglala Sioux by Black Elk* as told to John G. Neihardt, Lincoln, Nebraska: University of Nebraska Press, 1932, 1988. After I wrote this poem, a year later, I visited a "weaving studio" and discovered that this type of cloth is not woven on backstrap looms but, instead, produced on treadle looms, handled by men, in sweat shops that employ child labor. "Child labor" means children are not going to school; it means children in a room with air so thick with thread that your eyes itch after ten minutes, with air so thick with the thumping of looms that conversation is impossible. So now I need to write another poem for the small boys who spin the indigo yarn onto bobbins, their spinning wheels made of bicycle wheels.

Another View of Culture: She Explains Why She Loves Disney Cartoons

To understand the background of the civil war, see *Secret History: The CIA's Classified Account of Its Operations in Guatamala in 1952-54*, by Nick Cullather, Stanford University Press, 1999.

In the Name of the Daughter

The Dominican order was founded to combat heresy and to imitate the apostles by preaching. The parish clergy in Europe was poorly educated, sometimes not knowing the Latin used in the Mass. One priest who was reciting the mass with the words, "…in nomine patriae, et filiae, et spiritu sancti," or "in the name of the nation, the daughter, and the Holy Spirit." (This information comes from an article "Friars Preachers: The Dominican Order in the Middle Ages," www. florilegium. org/files/NICOLAA/Domin-Order-art.html.)

We Didn't Have the Words Then

The radio program quotes come from the book *A Fugitive Crosses His Tracks* byAksel Sandemose.

Vi skulle jo få glede av livet can be translated: *Of course we are supposed to find joy in this life.*

The Color of Hills and Water

tylwyth teg is the Welsh word for the faeries, literally, "fair kindred" or "ancestors."

glas is the first entry in *A Dictionary of the Welsh Language: blue, azure, sky-blue, greenish blue, sea green;* second entry: *green, grass-coloured, bluish green, verdant; unripe (of fruit); covered with green grass, clothed with verdure or foliage.*

menig y tylwyth teg is the Welsh word for foxglove means "glove of the faery" although I did not know that when I wrote this poem.

All I Knew About Wales Was That Grandpa Loved Ponies

The form of this poem was inspired by the work of Nazim Hikmet, "Things I Didn't Know I Loved."

My Grandpa Lloyd's parents, C.P. Lloyd and LaVisa Hobson, were married on horseback in Salem, Missouri, January 20, 1889.

The quote is from Woolf's description of the eclipse of June 30, 1927, published in *The Diary of Virginia Woolf, Volume Three, 1925-1930.*

About the Author

Roseann Lloyd's previous poetry collection, *War Baby Express,* Holy Cow! Press, received the Minnesota Book Award for Poetry in 1997. Her first collection of poetry, *Tap Dancing for Big Mom,* won the New Rivers Minnesota Voices Contest in 1985 and was published the next year. Lloyd has published other books in addition to her own poetry. The anthology she co-edited with Deborah Keenan, *Looking for Home: Women Writing about Exile* was awarded the American Book Award in 1991. Her translation of the contemporary Norwegian novel, *The House with the Blind Glass Windows,* written by Herbjørg Wassmo, was published by Seal Press. She has published nonfiction books with Harper/Hazelden, such as *JourneyNotes: Writing for Recovery and Spiritual Growth,* co-authored with Richard Solly. More information about her work and life can be found on her website, www.roseannlloyd.com. Lloyd currently resides in Minnesota; she was born in Springfield, Missouri, Queen City of the Ozarks.

Author's Note of Thanks

Books come into the world with the work of many hands. During part of the time I was working on this book, I received economic support from the following institutions: Minnesota State Arts Board Fellowship, Jerome Travel Grant 1998, Bush Artists' Fellowship, 1999. A special note of thanks to Mr. Bush, a fellow allergy sufferer, who made the money that supports the Bush Artists Fellows by going into business after his hay fever forced him off his family farm. If only all ailments produced such fortuitous blessings. These grants gave me the gift of time, a time to be quiet and separate from the workplace.

Thanks to the people who have supported my poems with places to write. To Liza Fourré of Art Workshops Guatemala, and Joan Drury, Norcroft: A Writing Retreat for Women, thank you for your ability to put dreams into action. To friends in other places, thank you for your hospitality, giving me a home away from home where I could rest and write.

A note of thanks to all who have given me feedback to these poems, especially manuscript readers Susan Cygnet, Brigitte Frase, Roberta Hill, Barbara Jones, Mary Junge, Deborah Keenan, Jan Levinsohn Milner, Toni McNaron, Jim Moore, Joe Paddock, Nancy Paddock, and Sheila Thomsen.

And for the beautiful art that graces the cover of this book, heart-felt thanks to Lisa McKhann for her creativity and kindness.

Continuing gratitude to my first teachers, Richard Hugo, Madeline DeFrees and Tess Gallagher, as well as gratitude to my own students whose love for poetry keeps it alive in our lives.

Last, joy and gratitude for the two Jims, Leos of the Heart: Jim Perlman, publisher extraordinaire, and Jim Smith, partner, calm friend every day.

For my family and friends, named and unnamed, much love for our shared lives.

May the Blessings Be.

Acknowledgements

Thanks to all the editors who published/performed my poems:

"A Dozen Reasons to Give Up Haggling Over the Price of Weavings," *Mount Voices*, 2001

"A Summer Day" and "Indigo," *LUNA: A Journal of Poetry and Translation*, Volume 6, 2003

"A Woman of the North Talking," *Borealis: The Magazine of Northern Literature, Art & Culture*, Volume 1, Number 1, January/February, 2002

"In the Name of the Daughter," *HEArt: human equity through art*, Volume 5, Number 1, Fall, 2001

"*Natt og Dag*: Return to Norway after 25 Years," *Sidewalks*, Number 19, Fall/Winter, 2000-2001

"*¿Qué Es?*" *Water~Stone: Hamline Literary Review*, Volume 3, Number 1, Fall 2000

"Massage," *Water~Stone: Hamline Literary Review*, Volume 4, Number 1, Fall 2001

"Midsummer Ghazal: July 2," forthcoming in *Water-Stone: Hamline Literary Review*

"Midsummer in the Midwest" and "Summer Dinner Party in Oslo," forthcoming in *Loonfeather*

"Movement," *The Midwest Quarterly: A Journal of Contemporary Thought*, Volume XLI, Number 2, Winter, 2000

"Recollect" and "Mørketiden: The Dark Time," *13th Moon*, Volume XVII, Numbers 1 & 2, 2002

"Resorting to Metaphor," *Sidewalks*, Volume 20, Summer, 2001

"Another Gift of the Northern Abolitionists," *Murphy Square 2001: Literary and Visual Arts Journal*, Augsburg College, Spring 2001

"Santa Clara Convent, Antigua, Guatemala," the 2000 Proceedings of the Red River Conference on World Literature, Exile of the Mind, "You've Done It Right the First Time, Darling" by Cass Dalglish, PhD., www.NDSV.nodak.edu/rrcwl (audio file) and published in *The Clackamas Literary Review*, Fall 2000, Volume IV, Issue II

"She Said," performed by poet April Lott in the winter performance of Twin Cities Women's Choir, Sundin Hall, Hamline University, February 2001, co-sponsored with SASE-The Write Place

"Still Point, July 25th" and "We Didn't Have the Words Then," <threecandles.org>, an online poetry journal, summer, 2001, and included in *Bell Beat: Selected Poetry, Lyrics, Comment*, a weekly online anthology <www.bellbeat.com/>, April 22, 2002

"Sorrow Comes in Spades," *Begin with a Blank Page: Norcroft: A Writing Retreat for Women, Tenth Anniversary Anthology*, The Norcroft Press, 2003

"What to Do The First Morning the Sun Comes Back," *The Minnesota Poetry Calendar*, 2000

"White Nights: A Woman of the North Talking," *Sidewalks*, Number 19, Fall/Winter, 2000-2001

"Winter Light," *Community Connections*, Winter, 2001